Just Wondering

40 Poems for Smart Kids (You)

Written by Suzanne Werkema
Illustrated by Tina Modugno

Just Wondering - 40 Poems for Smart Kids (You)
Copyright 2018 by Suzanne Werkema
Illustrated by Tina Modugno
Published 2018
All rights reserved.

Reproduction of individual poems and illustrations for personal, academic, or nonprofit use is allowed, providing author Suzanne Werkema and illustrator Tina Modugno are cited.
Reproduction for profit, whether of individual poems or illustrations or the entire book, is forbidden.

www.suzannewerkema.com
www.tinamodugno.com

ISBN-13: 978-0-9995945-0-6

*For My Mom and Dad
Cele and Alan Stark
With Deep Love and Gratitude*

People I (Might) Know

My Friend Chris	1
Family Reunion	3
The Boy in the Picture	5
Laryngitis	7
The Lie	8
Hoops	9
The Mushroom Hole	11
The Silverware's Lament	13
You Said What	15
Rootboy's Halloween	17

Science, Math, and Food

At the Worldwide Ice Cream Shop	18
Magic Diving Raisins	19
Riding the Line	21
I Tried to Grow a Redwood Tree	22
Gemelli	23
The Recipe	25
The Long Car Ride	27
School Projects	28

Outdoor Adventures

Be Ready to Duck	29
Sonnet for a Snow Mound	31
Summer Morning	32
The Boat Ride	33
Tracks	35
I Played in Poison Ivy	36

My Room
My Mess   37
Hangers   38
Aliens in My Room   39
I Miss My Room   41
Sleeping Late   42
Where's My Stuff   43

Thinking and Wondering
A Bad Day   45
I Dreamed I Flew   46
What If   47
Twelve A.M.   48
The Hideout   49
The Time Machine   51
Silence   52
Things That Never Happened   53
Just Wondering   55

And Finally
A Poem Is a Horrid Thing   57

My Friend Chris

My friend Chris can kick a ball
so high it disappears.
I can't kick a ball at all,
but I can swim for years.

Chris likes archaeology
and digging dinosaurs.
I like arachnology;
my spiders coat the floors.

When a tiger charges me,
Chris hauls it to the zoo.
When Chris topples from a tree,
I bring fresh legs and glue.

Chris has taught me how to build
a bicycle that flies.
I've helped Chris become quite skilled
at writing codes for spies.

Chris tells jokes that only Chris
and I can comprehend.
I make up tall tales like this,
and Chris knows how they end.

I'm like Chris flipped inside out.
Chris matches me the same.
We'll be friends till earthworms shout
and great white sharks are tame.

Family Reunion

I'm at a family
reunion, and with me
are my aunts, uncles, grand-
parents, four siblings, and
my niece's great-grandpas,
their nephews' new in-laws,
three-times-removed cousins,
nine babies, and dozens
here from my father's side,
there from my mother's side,
all saying, "Lovely to
see you again," but who
are they? Except for my
grandmas and grandpas, I
know just a few, and I
can't quite identify
these friendly people, their
faces, their names, or where
even one person lives.
Yet they're my relatives.

So now I'll quit eating
cookies, and start greeting
some of these people who
traveled so far just to
look in each other's eyes.
I'll find a kid my size,
ask this kid, "What's your name?
What's your most favorite game?"
We'll invite brothers in,
sisters and others, spin
stories, do flips, play ball,
adding in kids from all
sides of the family,
one giant team, then see
whether the grownups might
joke with us through the night.
After the party ends,
we will be cousin-friends.
Though we live far away,
we'll try our best to stay
buddies like we are today.

The Boy in the Picture

I found a photo, raggedy and old.
It shows a skater on a frozen pond.
He's dressed in heavy clothes against the cold.
He looks about my age or just beyond.
The boy is balancing on one ice skate,
his body crouching low, his arms spread wide,
his other leg stretched out in front of him,
his head upright, his back completely straight.
He's laughing as the camera sees him glide,
while other people watch him from the rim.

"That boy's your grandpa's grandpa," Mom explains.
"He loved to skate and swim, bike and canoe,
deliver newspapers, and then ride trains
cross-country to his college when he grew."
The old man died when Mom was twelve or so,
but she likes to remember. She says, "We
kids sat by him at home or in the car.
He listened when we spoke, played tic-tac-toe,
told funny stories. And a century
ago, he was a child just like you are."

"He carved the whistle on the kitchen shelf,"
she adds. "Gave it to me when I was ten.
I'm giving you that whistle for yourself,
to keep until you pass it on again."
The skating boy grins at the falling snow.
I wish I could have met him at my age.
I might have been his friend. I might have said,
"Let's skate. I want to learn the tricks you know."
I can't. But I see on this ragged page
my grandpa's grandpa as a boy instead.

Laryngitis

My mom had a cold, and she's better.
But something went wrong with her voice.
She whispers and grins and writes letters.
She doesn't have much of a choice.

She hands me my coat if it's raining.
She points to the beans on my plate.
She nods when she hears me complaining.
She taps on the clock if I'm late.

I want her to tell me a story.
I wish she could say, "How was school?"
This silence is starting to bore me.
I think laryngitis is cruel.

The Lie

My friend lied to me.
I cried when I found out.
I always thought she told the truth,
and I believed her.
But she lied.
She said she's sorry.
She said she'll never lie to me again.
She asked me to forgive her.
I said yes.
I'm not mad.
I still want to be friends.
But how do I know
she's speaking truth?
What if her words
are just another lie?
How can I trust her?
I hope in days to come
she'll tell me many truthful things
and nothing false,
and maybe then
I'll trust my friend again.
For now, I tell myself
she didn't mean to lie,
and what she says today
is likely true.

Hoops

The hoop I like best hangs outside my garage. Some
days all of my teammates shoot baskets till night.
My mom, at my age, preferred hoops that hung down from
her ears, hoops of silver, eye-catching and bright.

Her mama, my grandma, loved twirling her hula
hoop 'round on her waist without letting it droop.
Her mom, my great-gram, played croquet after school. The
ball spun 'cross the grass through each upside-down hoop.

Before this, *her* mother, a young artist, used flat
embroidery hoops to hold stitches she sewed.
Her mom as a child had a large wooden hoop that
she pushed with a stick as it rolled down the road.

And *her* mother wore a hoop skirt ringed with whalebone,
to follow the fashion of girls of her day.
Including my b-ball hoop, seven kinds, well-known,
were owned by these kids and used in their own way.

My family has always liked hoops since before my
great-great-great-great-grandma could crawl on her knees.
And these seven hoops will be eight if someday I
hear my daughter saying, "I want that hoop, please."

The Mushroom Hole

In our basement there's a small dark room,
six by ten feet, concrete walls and floor,
one bare ceiling bulb to break the gloom.

"It's a mushroom hole," our neighbor said.
"Grow some mushrooms there." We don't. We store
stacks of old forgotten junk instead.

Every wall is lined with wooden shelves
jammed with bags and boxes packed with stuff
rarely used, just secrets for ourselves.

Giggling, we paw through the mess. We find
curiosities and gear and fluff
needed in the past, now left behind:

> shoes with bird shapes carved into the heels,
> decorated Christmas cookie tins,
> tricycles with cards clipped to the wheels,
>
> extra birthday plates, thin red balloons,
> picnic baskets, checkers, snorkel fins,
> cuckoo clocks, a set of baby spoons,
>
> swirly skirts with poodles on the front,
> stilts, a street sign, snowshoes, bowling pins,
> odds and ends to fill a morning's hunt.

What we never find are pearls or cash,
diamonds, gold doubloons from ships that wrecked.
Nothing valuable hides in the stash.

All we seek is fun. Our goal's not big.
In our mushroom hole we don't expect
buried treasure. We just like to dig.

The Silverware's Lament

On days when my sister and I have a fight
and stomp through the kitchen to prove that we're right,
if I set the table for supper, I hear
the silverware moaning and clinking with fear.

> "No, don't put us near her.
> We dislike your sister.
> We want you to choose us.
> Oh please don't refuse us."

The knives, forks, and spoons that I give Dad and Mom
all look disappointed but keep themselves calm.
The ones at my plate shout a joyful "Hooray!"
But those at my sister's plate wail in dismay.

"We're ruined! We'll never
be happy, not ever.
Please don't turn and leave us.
Come back and retrieve us."

On days when my sister and I get along,
play games and tell stories and nothing goes wrong,
the silverware's mute as I spread it around –
no begging, no groaning, not one single sound.

You Said What?
(a poem for two people)

"Last night I gave my dog a bath."

    "Last month our bathtub overflowed."

"She'd gone six months. I did the math."

    "Six rooms got soaked before it slowed."

"She whimpered when I soaked her skin."

    "We whimpered when we knew our plight."

"She yelped and fought but knew I'd win."

    "We fought the flood and cleaned all night."

"All clean, she romped around the floor."

"We're getting our new floor today."

"Today she'll run in dirt once more."

"Now when we run a bath, we stay."

"You stayed to win six bathroom doors?"

"You fought six months but you're not hurt?"

"Your tub blew up but not the floors?"

"Your dog does math and then eats dirt?"

Rootboy's Halloween

My cousin Rootboy said, "You know,
in Roottown no one trick-or-treats.
If you and I together go,
we'll each collect a bag of sweets."

I dressed in pirate garb. He stayed
himself, all roots, no mouth, no eyes.
My neighbors crowed, "This rootboy's made
the year's best Halloween disguise."

At home, as I poured out our snacks,
he moaned, "I can't eat candy, Bud."
So I devoured my Cracker Jacks
and Rootboy drank a bowl of mud.

At the Worldwide Ice Cream Shop

"Please, I'd like two scoops to go –
chocolate chunk and cookie dough."

*"Sure, kid. Now what currency
will you pay with? Will it be*

*dollar, dirham, lari, baht,
kwanza, kwacha, lek, manat,*

*shilling, shequel, pound, lempira,
florin, franc, pa'anga, lira,*

*naira, nakfa, kip, rupiah,
peso, pula, kroon, ouguiya,*

*euro, escudo, yuan,
ruble, rand, afghani, won?*

*We take other moneys, too.
Any kind. It's up to you."*

"Thanks, but choosing isn't hard.
I'll pay with my new gift card."

Magic Diving Raisins

Our science class experiment seemed small:
First get club soda. Pour some in a glass.
Drop several raisins in. Watch as they fall
and rise, thanks to carbon dioxide gas.

The bubbles fill the raisins' wrinkled skin
and lift them to the surface. Bubbles pop.
The raisins sink. More bubbles nestle in.
The raisins bob for hours before they stop.

At home I told my sister, five years old,
"I have twelve magic diving raisins. See?"
I showed her the experiment. She rolled
her eyes but said, "Would they do that for me?"

I wandered off to play. She stuck her hand
inside the glass and pulled the raisins up,
to learn if they would follow her command,
and dive in something deeper than a cup.

She ran down to the basement. Mom was there
to paint cement walls pocked with dents and bumps.
The roller was as furry as a bear.
The paint was thick as pudding filled with lumps.

A big five-gallon pail held all the paint.
My sister sneaked the raisins in the pail.
They floated, but she stirred without complaint.
They vanished, and she saw the test would fail.

She came to me to ask what she'd done wrong.
I said, "You need a carbonated drink.
The bubbles make the raisins move along.
Carbon dioxide helps them rise and sink."

Mom finished up the job. She didn't spot the raisins in the paint. She used it all. That's why until today our basement's got twelve magic diving raisins on the wall.

Riding the Line

A straight line on a page hits the edge and gets stuck.
Though the lunch line at school stretches long, it does end.
The halfway line in soccer must stop and not bend.
But a line in geometry has better luck.

'Cause this line goes forever and ever both ways,
without breaking or curving while streaking on by.
It pokes clear through the walls, through the clouds, through the sky,
to the point where the universe runs out of days.

So my plan for exploring the reaches of space
needs a plain simple line aiming out beyond Mars.
To see asteroids, galaxies, wormholes, and stars,
I'll just hop on the line to the farthest-out place.

I Tried to Grow a Redwood Tree

I tried to grow a redwood tree.
I planted one small seed.
I gave the dirt
a healthy squirt
to satisfy its need.

I watched the brown soil carefully
to see the seedling sprout.
The sunlight there
was fairly rare,
the rainfall more like drought.

I guess a tree's a mystery,
'cause nothing came to pass.
Instead of trees
I now grow these:
potatoes in a glass.

Gemelli
(jeh-MEH-lee)

Spaghetti is great, macaroni first-rate, but
I eat them so often they're boring.
I like pasta best when it's shaped to suggest what
new plans I can make for exploring.

Rotelle looks like spokes and wheels on my bike, while
stelline is stars, only thinner.
Farfalle's shape brings to mind butterfly wings. I'll
examine these things after dinner.

The pasta that makes my foot slam on the brakes? It's
gemelli - two strings twisted tightly.
It spirals away almost like DNA, bits
of secret code hidden inside me.

My DNA floats in each cell, tiny notes to
direct how my body's created.
I got the whole crop from my mom and my pop, who
resemble me, since we're related.

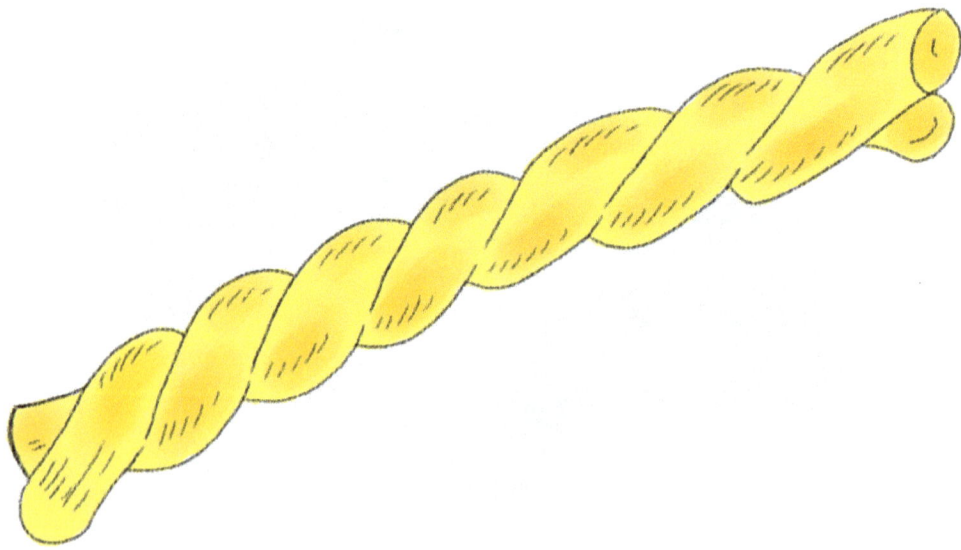

My code says my eyes are dark brown, and my size must
be small, but I'm strong since forever.
I sang at age two. My tongue curls like a U. Plus
I'm left-handed, freckled, and clever.

And DNA codes work in tigers and toads, in
all critters and plants, not just humans.
It's why my cats play, why my dad's hair turned gray, skin
can stretch, and old trees can start new ones.

I hope to learn loads of these DNA codes. So
I eat hearty plates of gemelli.
Can pasta explain why my feet need my brain? No,
but still it feels good in my belly.

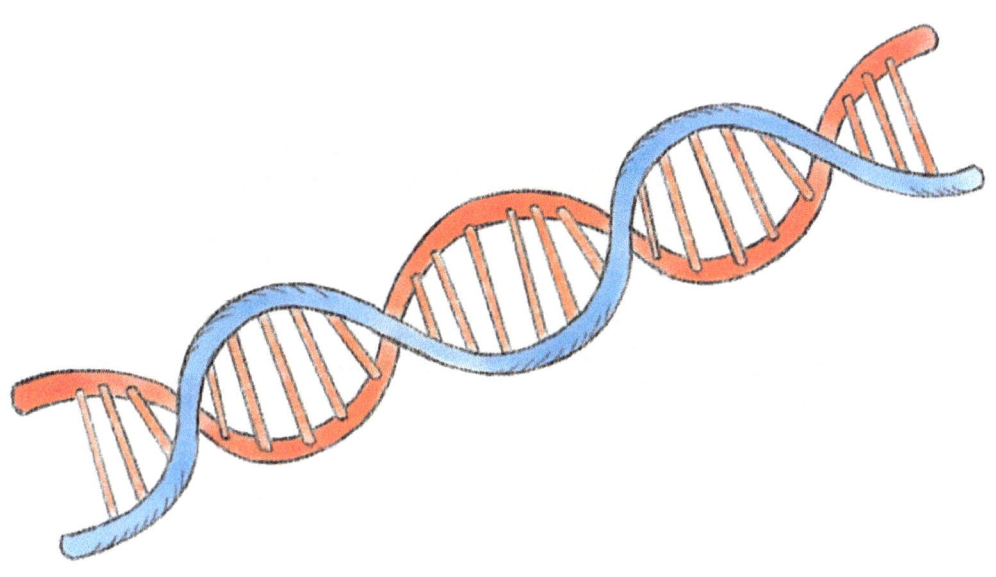

Rotelle = roh-TEH-leh
Stelline = steh-LEE-neh
Farfalle = far-FAH-leh

The Recipe

My grandma has an antique book
that teaches how to sew and cook,
clean walls and wicks, boil toast to drink,
make medicines and soap and ink.

The book's a hundred ten years old,
almost too delicate to hold,
with recipes for real mincemeat,
peach marmalade, and soused pigs' feet.

The recipe I'd like to make
is this one, for a bridal cake:
Of sweet fresh butter, take four pounds.
Add four pounds flour. Beat into mounds.

Stir two pounds sugar in the mix,
and for each pound of flour, add six,
yes, twenty-four – two dozen! – eggs,
also an ounce of ground nutmegs,

a tablespoon of lemon juice,
then blend it all till smooth as mousse.
What kind of pan? How hot to cook?
When is it done? How should it look?

The recipe just stops right there,
as if the cook must be aware
of how to bake things for a bride
without becoming glassy-eyed.

A century ago, perhaps
books didn't fill in all the gaps.
Kids practiced with their family
or learned experimentally.

I like to solve hard problems, too,
and figure out what's best to do.
But for this bridal cake, I need
complete instructions I can read.

The Long Car Ride

I'm on an endless car ride. I suppose
I will be old and gray before it's done.
I've read my books and watched my videos,
and now there's nothing else to do that's fun.

I wish I'd brought some cookie dough. I could
break chunks off and then shape them into flowers.
I'd bake them in the hot sun on the hood,
then munch my floral treats to pass the hours.

I'd share the rest with kids in other cars,
by flinging cookies to them, 'cross the air
and through their open windows, in small jars,
all day and night and week and – hey, we're there!

School Projects

At school this year it seems to me the spotlight is on food.
Our projects and materials are baked, stirred, chopped, dried, stewed.

We counted up a million beans to fill a hundred crates.
We found that bread rots slower if the dough is mixed with dates.
We built a model of the Taj Mahal with sugar cubes.
We blew up a balloon with gas from veggies in test tubes.
We sold a ton of trail mix to help victims of earthquakes.
We weighed, then melted, weighed again a pot of chocolate flakes.
We sang about medieval feasts where birds flew out of pies.
We hammered sticks of cinnamon to make them pulverize.
We studied recipes and cooked a taco salad snack.
We sculpted clay to look like maple pancakes in a stack.
We drew a map of Europe using carrot sticks and cheese.
We forced a clock to tell time with potato batteries.

I like to play with food, but all these projects make me drool.
I'm ravenously hungry by the time I leave the school.

Be Ready to Duck

We went to a pro baseball game Friday night,
my uncle and I. We sat just to the right
of home plate, at field level, hoping to win.
Before long, our team had two runs batted in.

But some of the batters hit high-flying fouls.
The fans gnawed their hot dogs. We heard groans and growls,
except when foul balls left the diamond and soared
up into the seats. Then the happy crowd roared.

Soon one of our best batters came to the plate.
He struck once. He struck twice. He just couldn't wait.
He swung, and his bat flew clear out of his hands
and shot like a missile straight into the stands.

I watched it speed closer, aimed right at my head.
I wanted to duck. I was frozen with dread.
Like lightning my uncle jumped sideways to catch
the missile. My head caught not even a scratch.

For now this bat hangs on my wall like a prize.
I practice each day with a bat more my size.
I'm learning to hit far and fast, but I try
as hard as I can not to let the bat fly.

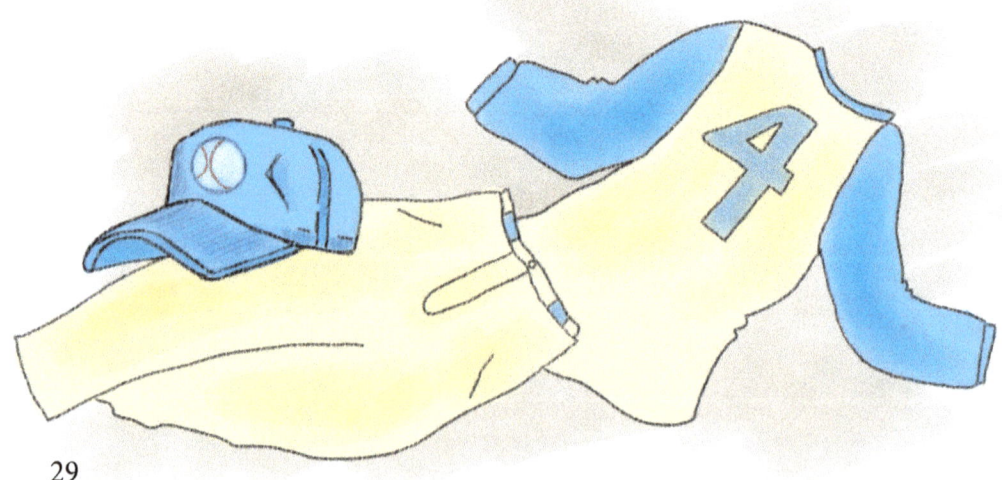

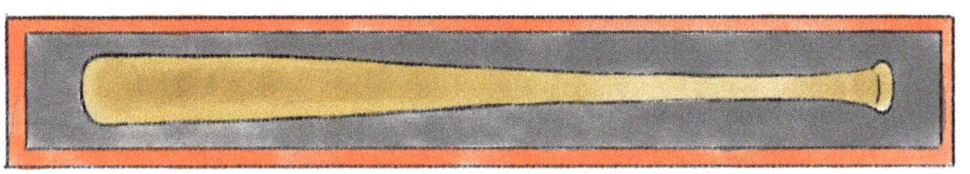

Sonnet for a Snow Mound

A wintry blizzard dumped three feet of snow.
Dad snow-blew some into a giant mound
that reached the roof. He climbed the mound to blow
the heavy drifts from our roof to the ground.

Dad let us climb up with him. We could see
our whole street and the river, miles away.
We yelled, "Hello down there!" Then Dad and we
climbed to our rooftop lookout every day.

A warm wind came – the January thaw.
The snow mound melted down to half its height.
The roof rose up, unreachable. We saw
our lookout fade completely from our sight.

So now we watch the weather, night and noon,
in hopes a wintry blizzard will come soon.

Summer Morning

Summer morning: through closed eyelids I see sunshine.
Should I get up now or sleep some more?
Half awake, I stretch and catch the scent of white pine,
as a ski boat cruises near the shore.

This vacation cottage sits beside the sand. I'll
spend the whole day playing in the lake,
swimming, fishing, finding shells, and building moats, while
learning how to ski and jump the wake.

Now my brain's alert. Someone is cutting grass. A
mower's what I heard – no boat, it seems.
I'm at home in my own bed, and sad to find the
sand and lake were just my summer dreams.

But the mower tells me there's a big yard waiting.
I can run, turn somersaults, play ball,
spend the whole day bicycling and roller skating,
and I'll hardly miss the beach at all.

The Boat Ride

The captain calls, "Welcome aboard!"
He's my friend's dad. I'm on their boat.
The motor revs. We launch out toward
the river, for a day afloat.

A heron with an S-shaped neck
waits on a log among the reeds.
As we glide by, he leaves his deck
and flies beside us, matching speeds.

To cross a barge's wake, we reach
thick rolls of water, rough and wide.
We rise – ploosh! – to the top of each,
then drop – splat! – down the other side.

A kid my size stands fishing by
a grownup with a tackle box.
The kid's rod bends and jerks, lifts high.
A shiny fish lands on the rocks.

We cruise into a sheltered bay
and anchor. We jump off the stern
to swim, find shells, and kick up spray,
till sunset says we must return.

The river's different now. It flows
not smoothly, but in bumpy chops.
My legs are tired. A night wind blows.
But I hope this boat never stops.

Tracks

I know a word that's flexible and fun.
It has a bunch of meanings, not just one.
The word is track, and here's a list of ways
to track how different tracks may spend their days.

Trains speed on railroad tracks from town to town.
Detectives try to track bank robbers down.
The tracks of tires leave patterns on the street.
Dogs track through living rooms with muddy feet.

Strong runners race on tracks to win a prize.
The tracks of comets streak across the skies.
Deer tracks lead from the water to the brush.
And dirt bikes track through forests in a rush.

My favorite tracks of all the kinds I know?
The tracks my sled makes in the winter snow.

I Played in Poison Ivy

I played in poison ivy.
My skin grew rough and red.
I scratched at first; the rash got worse.
I itched from toes to head.

I rubbed on special lotion.
The bumps have gone away.
A poison ivy patch is my
least favorite place to play.

My Mess

My mother says my bedroom's messy nine times out of ten.
I clean, but in a nanosecond it's a wreck again.
My mother says my room's become a private garbage heap.
But everything I own's important stuff I need to keep.
My theory is that my possessions jump around at night.
My mother says that's no excuse for leaving things a fright.
I have a plan, if Mom agrees. I'll type her shopping lists,
fold clothes and wash the dog if she'll forget my room exists.

Hangers

Why are hangers so persnickety?
Keeping them in line is such a chore.
I hang up my clothes, then clickety-
clack, I hear them crumble to the floor.

Hangers shouldn't be so rickety,
tangling on the rod or where they fell.
I don't mean to sound too pickety,
but those hangers make me want to yell.

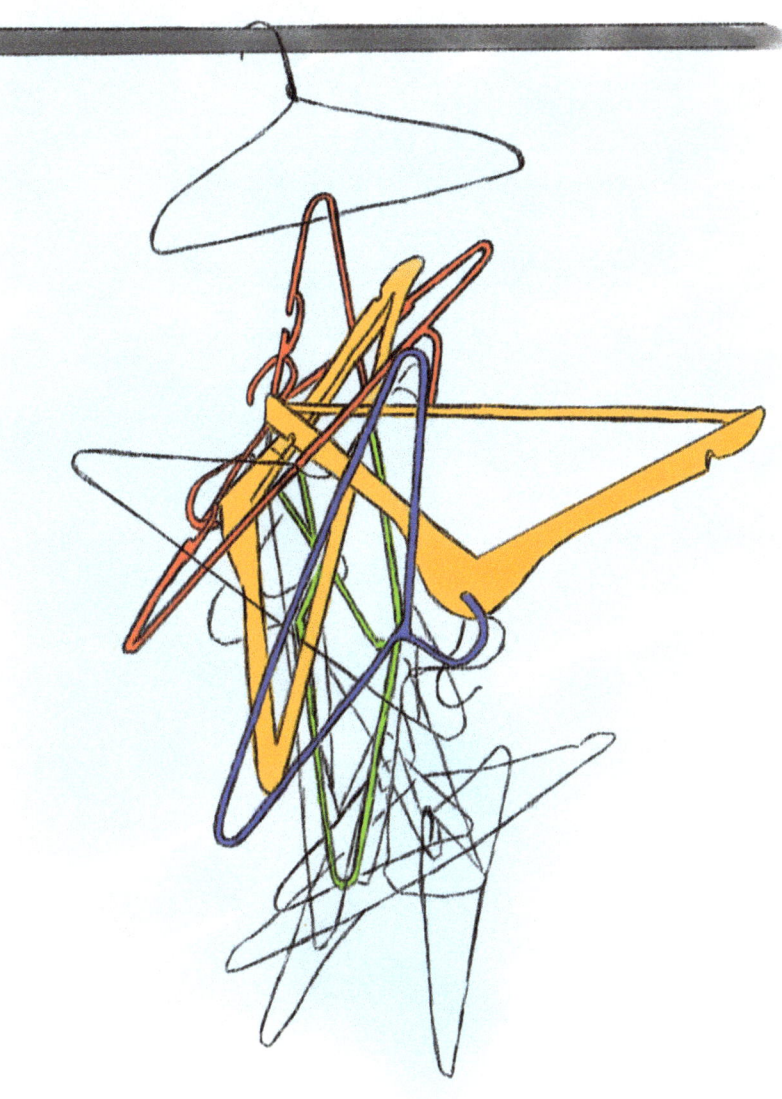

Aliens in My Room

I always thought if creatures came
to earth from distant galaxies,
they'd lock me up and change my name
and steal my bike and feed me fleas.

But last night as a rustling wind
awoke me, I heard something purr.
Ten tiny aliens bounced in
like ping-pong balls made out of fur.

They rolled around, then sprouted heads
and fuzzy legs and tails. They twirled
and sprang from chair to desk to bed,
exploring in their brand-new world.

I stretched my fingers out to pet
their fur. They raised their paws in play.
They batted at my hand, and let
me touch them. Then they hopped away.

They rolled back up and purred once more.
I guess they couldn't stay, because
they vanished, leaving on my floor
a single tuft of soft green fuzz.

I Miss My Room

We moved. My new room feels so strange.
Perhaps someday I'll like it more.
Outside my window grows a tree
I'll climb, and I see kids next door.

But my old bedroom was my home.
It fit me like a second skin –
my planet, castle, forest, boat,
or any world my brain could spin.

I knew my way round every bump
and color, every speck of space,
and anywhere I looked was like
a mirror, showing my own face.

The stuff I use we packed and brought.
The bed and desk and clothes are mine.
My friends will visit. But the room
that felt like me, we left behind.

Sleeping Late

I am sleeping late.
Deep snow drifts cover the streets,
and school is cancelled.

Where's My Stuff?

Two years ago my dad was gardening,
and in the dirt he lost his wedding ring.
Today in that same garden, planting seeds,
he found his wedding ring beneath the weeds.
If Dad can find his ring, then where's the stuff
I've lost? I think I've waited long enough.

What happened to the coin from Mexico?
The birthday wrapping paper and the bow?
The felt pen that drew lines of shiny gold?
The picture of my dog at one month old?
The painted model car my brother made?
The stack of baseball cards I used to trade?

Right now I'm pawing round my closet floor,
just like I've done a hundred times before.
I never find the things I lose, but still
I always hope this time perhaps I will.
This closet's a disaster. I'm too late
 to see my stuff again. It's gone. But wait –

A curly bow of ribbons red and blue
is peeking from behind my outgrown shoe.
A picture of a dog with puppy eyes
is mixed inside a box of art supplies.
Is there a chance I'm finding things at last?
Did I just overlook them in the past?

I'll search again, on shelves, in books I've read,
in drawers, in bags, and underneath my bed.
My missing treasures may be in one spot
or scattered wide throughout the house. If not,
I'll do what my dad did. I'll stay alert,
wait two more years, and find them in the dirt.

A Bad Day

I'm glad this day is finally done.
I didn't have a bit of fun.
I wiped a felt-pen on my shirt;
I dropped my sandwich in the dirt;
I failed a mathematics test;
my teammates claimed I'm just a pest;
my homework took a century;
my mom decided "No TV";
my sister said I'm a disgrace;
my dog refused to sniff my face.
So now I think I'll go to bed
and push this day out of my head.
Tomorrow I'll have energy
to try again to just be me.
And nothing will get in the way,
for it will be a brand new day.

I Dreamed I Flew

I dreamed I flew,
my arms spread wide and steady,
my body weightless,
stretched out flat,
an inch above the calm bright sea.
I flew swiftly,
without effort,
without fear,
as soft air,
silent, fresh, and warm,
slid past my face.
I flew for hours,
far from land,
amazed the sea stayed still,
amazed I stayed aloft,
amazed my thoughts stayed
gentle as the wind.
I hope I have that dream again.

What If?

What if a tadpole grew into a goat?
What if an anchor decided to float?
What if an eyeball found out it could hear?
Would this be funny or something to fear?

What if fake moustaches fell from the sky?
What if the windows all started to cry?
What if our cars sprouted feathers and wings?
How would we handle these bothersome things?

We could crochet tadpole hair into socks,
tie floating anchors to big cement blocks,
hold ringing telephones up to our eyes,
wear the fake moustaches as a disguise.

We could bring tissues to comfort the glass,
fill up our gas tanks with birdseed, not gas.
We could get used to these changes somehow.
But aren't things better the way they are now?

Twelve A.M.

Midnight.

I'm still awake.

My clock glows through darkness.

I've heard tales of late-night strangeness.

Twelve o'clock brings mysteries and danger.

I slink down beneath the blankets.

Waiting. Nothing happens.

I fall asleep.

Midnight.

The Hideout

My family, on vacation,
stopped for dinner at a restaurant
in an old stone farmhouse on a country road.
The sign read, "Built in 1702. Try our world famous apple pie."
The host said, "Please seat yourselves
at any table on the second floor.
And on your way upstairs,
check the slave hideout built into the wall."
We walked halfway up and looked.
The hideout was a cavern in the thick stone wall,
an empty space the size of a refrigerator lying down.
Wooden doors once blocked the open side,
to make it seem a cupboard for extra pots.
Now there's glass instead, a window to a dangerous, secret place.
The slaves who hid inside this cave were runaways
fleeing cruelty, fleeing violence,
weary of being owned just like a bowl or a chair.
When they escaped, they had to hide.
Their owners tracked their every step,
to capture them and make them slaves again.
In safe-houses, in holes in walls,
in barns and attics, cellars and sheds
of people who considered slavery wrong,
the runaways stayed a day, a week, or more,
until the chasers took another route.
Then the slaves could move again
toward the next stop on the underground railroad,
their freedom road.
We looked at the hideout, my family and I, and I thought,
What if we'd been slaves,
cramped and frightened in this little cave,
knowing if we crept outside
someone might drag us back to bondage?

If I were a slave, I'd wonder
why other kids laugh gladly in the yard,
why dogs bark when they feel like barking,
why even mosquitoes choose whose arms to bite.
I hope we would have run.
I hope we would have journeyed,
station to station, night to night,
ending finally where we didn't have to hide.

The Time Machine

I'm buckled tight inside my time machine.
The dial picks an unknown year and place.
Lights flash. For half a moment I'm between
two worlds. I exit to a strange new space.

I'm at a beach. The people on the sand
are boarding rafts to sail across the sea,
past curved horizons to a distant land.
One waiting raft has saved a spot for me.

Some people think the sea's a cliff. They fear
we'll sail straight off and fall into a pit
or get devoured by beasts and disappear.
But I want to explore and never quit.

My time machine has dialed me a pledge:
a future and a hope beyond the edge.

Silence

In a quiet room,
a lulled and tranquil room,
with no one stirring,
nothing whirring,
not a chirp,
the silence hums.
You must listen carefully
for the noise,
the gentle brushing sound.
What could it be?
Perhaps it's atoms scraping past each other,
perhaps electrons spurting energy,
or tiny sprites of air tiptoeing by.
Perhaps it's memories bumping other memories,
or wishes rubbing wishes as they meet.
Perhaps children in a far galaxy long ago
yelled "Anybody out there?"
and traces of their voices just arrived.
Perhaps it is God whispering.
Who knows?
If you hold very still and listen,
in the quietest of hushed places,
you will hear.

Things That Never Happened

I feared I'd fail my science test.
I passed it with a B.
I worried that I'd never swim.
I now dive easily.
I knew I'd catch the flu, but I
stayed healthy all the same.
I feared my friends were angry, till
they let me join their game.

I studied for my science test.
That's maybe why I passed.
I signed up for a swimming class.
I learned to float at last.
I stayed away from sick kids, and
I washed my hands a lot.
I asked my friends, "Is something wrong?"
They said, "We just forgot."

I get concerned quite often, but
it's more or less a waste.
The horrors that my brain expects
are frequently erased.
Sometimes I can prevent them, or
they simply don't occur.
And then the things I fear become
the things that never were.

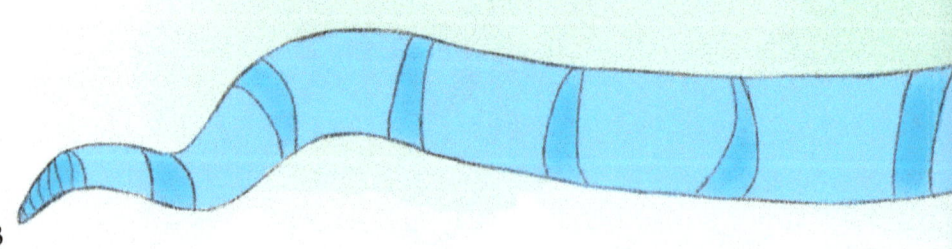

Just Wondering

Why do crabs walk sideways?
Why do dogs have dreams?
Why do people love their cars?
Why do candles come in jars?
Why do fish survive in frozen streams?

How does toast melt butter?
How do zippers break?
How do we catch yawns from cats?
How does vinegar trap gnats?
How do cooks know how much food to make?

What's the biggest number?
What's the newest game?
What do night owls do all day?
What sports do work horses play?
What if I could choose a different name?

Who created oatmeal?
Who saw what I did?
Who made purple red plus blue?
Who tells rulers what to do?
Who was Grandma when she was a kid?

Where's your secret hideout?
Where do gnomes put trash?
Where's my jacket with the hood?
Where would I live if I could?
Where does lightning go after the flash?

When will I get older?
When was long ago?
When did they invent balloons?
When did Saturn get its moons?
When will I learn all there is to know?

A Poem Is a Horrid Thing

A poem is a horrid thing,
all fancy, frilly, fluttering.
I want my words red-hot and bold,
not sappy, simpering, and old.

Hey, did you know gorillas fly
in paper planes around the sky,
then slide back down on sprinkler spray
and hide until you look away?

Next Saturday, let's go explore
the land beneath my bedroom floor.
It's filled with trolls. They'll let us sail
the ocean on their giant snail.

When I grow up, I think I might
invent a food that gives off light.
Then if my brother sneaks a snack,
I'll see it glowing through his back.

I like to hear this kind of stuff,
but poems just aren't fun enough.
So till the moon outshines the sun,
I'll never read a single one.

www.ingramcontent.com/pod-product-compliance
Lightning Source LLC
Chambersburg PA
CBHW051553010526
44118CB00022B/2698